HOUSTON TEXANS

BY JOSH ANDERSON

Stride
An Imprint of The Child's World®
childsworld.com

The Child's World
childsworld.com

Published by The Child's World®
800-599-READ • www.childsworld.com

Photography Credits
Cover: © Scott Winters / Icon Sportswire / Newscom; page 1: © Africa Studio / Shutterstock; page 3: © Bob Levey / Stringer / Getty Images; page 5: © Ronald Martinez / Stringer / Getty Images; page 6: © Ronald Martinez / Stringer / Getty Images; page 9: © Bob Levey / Stringer / Getty Images; page 10: © Chris Graythen / Staff / Getty Images; page 11: © stevezmina1 / Getty Images; page 12: © Carmen Mandato / Staff / Getty Images; page 12: © Christian Petersen / Staff / Getty Images; page 13: © Leslie Plaza Johnson/Icon Sportswire / Newscom; page 13: © Bob Levey / Stringer / Getty Images; page 14: © Bob Levey / Stringer / Getty Images; page 15: © Daniel Dunn/Icon Sportswire / Newscom; page 16: © Scott Halleran / Staff / Getty Images; page 16: © Wesley Hitt / Stringer / Getty Images; page 17: © Tom Pennington / Staf / Getty Images; page 17: © Andy Lyons / Staff / Getty Images; page 18: © Ronald Martinez / Stringer / Getty Images; page 18: © Scott Halleran / Staff / Getty Images; page 19: © Bob Levey / Stringer / Getty Images; page 19: © Christian Petersen / Staff / Getty Images; page 20: © Carmen Mandato / Stringer / Getty Images; page 20: © Carmen Mandato / Staff / Getty Images; page 21: © Bob Levey / Stringer / Getty Images; page 21: © Gregory Shamus / Staff / Getty Images; page 22: © Bob Levey / Stringer / Getty Images; page 23: © Scott Halleran / Staff / Getty Images; page 23: © stevezmina1 / Getty Images; page 25: © Thomas B. Shea / Stringer / Getty Images; page 26: © Thomas B. Shea / Stringer / Getty Images; page 29: © Jeff Gross / Staff / Getty Images

ISBN Information
9781503857773 (Reinforced Library Binding)
9781503860506 (Portable Document Format)
9781503861862 (Online Multi-user eBook)
9781503863224 (Electronic Publication)

LCCN 2021952693

Printed in the United States of America

BRINGING THE WORLD TO YOUNG READERS 19 68

TABLE OF CONTENTS

GO TEXANS!

The Houston Texans compete in the National Football **League's** (NFL's) American Football Conference (AFC). They play in the AFC South **division**, along with the Indianapolis Colts, Jacksonville Jaguars, and Tennessee Titans. Fans in Houston were lucky in 2002 when the NFL granted the city an **expansion team**. The Texans are the most recent team to join the league. While it took the team a while to earn their first trip to the **playoffs**, they made the postseason six times between 2011 and 2019. Let's learn more about the Texans!

AFC SOUTH DIVISION

Houston Texans

Indianapolis Colts

Jacksonville Jaguars

Tennessee Titans

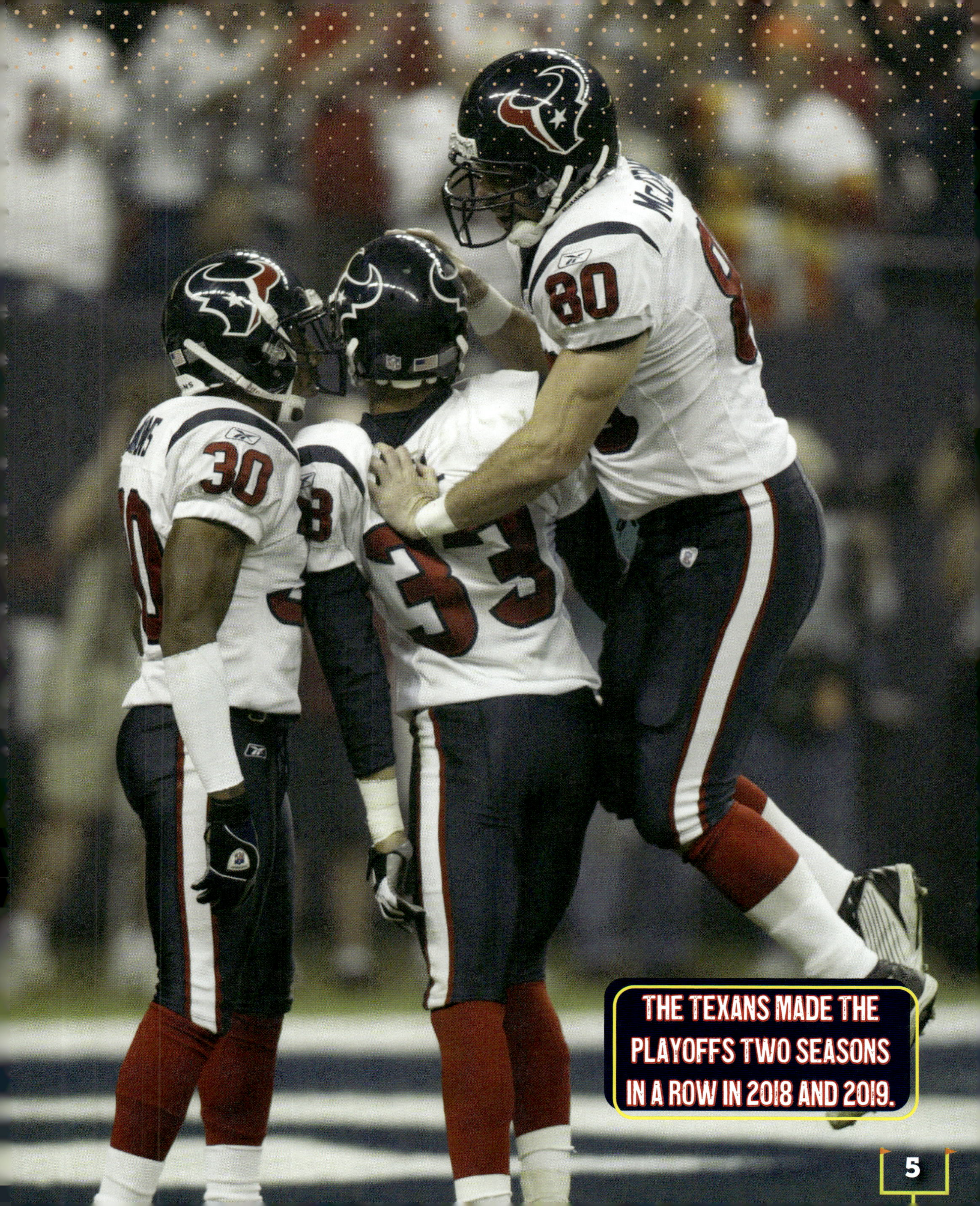

THE TEXANS MADE THE PLAYOFFS TWO SEASONS IN A ROW IN 2018 AND 2019.

TEXANS

BECOMING THE TEXANS

From 1960 to 1996, the city of Houston, Texas, was home to the Oilers. The Oilers left the city after the 1996 season and moved to Tennessee. They became the Tennessee Titans. In 2002, the NFL gave Houston back an NFL team and the Texans were born. Other names considered for the team were the Apollos, Bobcats, Stallions, and Wildcatters. The Texans had their first winning season in 2009 and made the playoffs for the first time in 2011. The team has never won the **Super Bowl**, but fans of the team hope their first championship is right around the corner.

DAVID CARR STARTED EVERY GAME AS QUARTERBACK DURING THE TEXANS' FIRST SEASON IN 2002.

BY THE NUMBERS

SIX
division titles for the Texans

SIX
head coaches in Texans team history

416
points scored by the team in 2012—a Texans record!

12
wins for the Texans in 2012

THE TEXANS ARE ONE OF 12 NFL TEAMS THAT HAVE NEVER WON A SUPER BOWL.

TEXANS FANS SHOWED UP IN RECORD NUMBERS TO WATCH THEIR TEAM DEFEAT THE CINCINNATI BENGALS IN THE PLAYOFFS IN 2012.

GAME DAY

For their entire history, the Texans have played their home games at NRG **Stadium**. NRG Stadium has a roof that can be opened or closed in about seven minutes. Approximately 72,000 fans can fit inside to watch the Texans play. The digital display boards in each end zone are the second largest in any NFL stadium. Fans can see the action from any seat. In 2017, NRG Stadium hosted Super Bowl 51 between the New England Patriots and the Atlanta Falcons.

We're Famous!

The Texans were featured on season 10 of HBO's series *Hard Knocks*. The show features moments from the team's training camp and preseason as they work to choose their 53-man roster and get ready for the NFL season ahead. The Texans didn't seem to be distracted by all the cameras around. They finished the season 9–7 and made the playoffs that year.

UNIFORM

BLUE

WHITE

Truly Weird

After lining up in a punt formation during a 2021 game against the New England Patriots, Texans punter Cameron Johnston ran up to the line of scrimmage. The Texans tried to show the Patriots they were going to run a real play instead of punt the ball. Then, when the Patriots defense adjusted, Johnston tried to move back and punt the ball. But he didn't move far enough back and kicked the ball right into the helmet of one of his teammates. The ball flew out of bounds, and the result of the punt was zero yards.

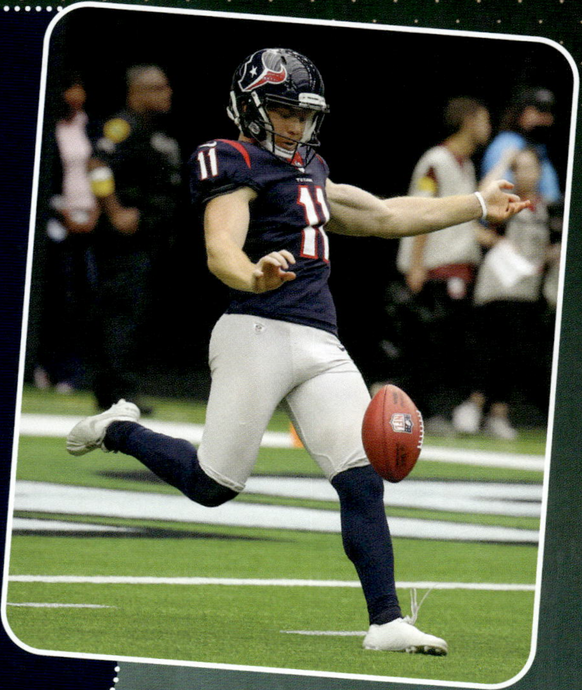

Alternate Jersey

Sometimes teams wear an alternate jersey that is different from their home and away jerseys. It might be a bright color or have a unique theme. For a Monday night game against the Baltimore Ravens in 2010, the Texans wore their all-red uniforms. The new look proved unlucky, though. The Texans lost the game.

TEXAN FANS ARE PROUD OF THEIR TEAM AND THEIR STATE, AND THEY FIND CREATIVE WAYS TO SHOW THEIR PRIDE AT HOME GAMES.

TEAM SPIRIT

Going to a game at NRG Stadium can be a ton of fun. Some of the most passionate fans sit in the "Bull Pen" behind the north end zone. Fans in this section often stand for most of the game. They lead songs and chants for the rest of the people in the stadium. The Houston Texans Cheerleaders root on the team at every home game. They're joined by the team's mascot, Toro. In Spanish, *toro* means "bull." He's a huge costumed bull who helps get the fans excited.

TORO

HEROES OF HISTORY

Arian Foster

Running Back | 2009–2015

Foster is the Texans' career leader, with 6,472 rushing yards and 54 rushing **touchdowns**. In 2010, Foster led the NFL with 1,616 yards rushing yards, along with 16 touchdowns. His career average of 81.6 rushing yards per game is 16th in NFL history. He was chosen for the **Pro Bowl** four times.

DeAndre Hopkins

Wide Receiver | 2013–2019

Hopkins finished with more than 1,000 yards in five of his seven seasons in Houston. During that time, he totaled 8,602 receiving yards and 54 touchdowns. Hopkins led the league with 13 receiving touchdowns in 2017. He was chosen for the Pro Bowl four times as a member of the Texans.

Andre Johnson

Wide Receiver | 2003–2014

Johnson is 11th in NFL history, with 14,185 receiving yards. He twice led the league in catches and also led the league in receiving yards twice. During his time with the Texans, Johnson had more than 1,000 receiving yards in a season seven times. He was chosen for seven Pro Bowls.

Mario Williams

Defensive End | 2006–2011

Williams was a star at North Carolina State University. Then the Texans chose him first overall in the 2006 NFL Draft. "Super Mario" anchored the Texans' defensive line for half a decade. He's third on the team's all-time list with 53 **sacks**. Williams was chosen for two Pro Bowls as a member of the Texans.

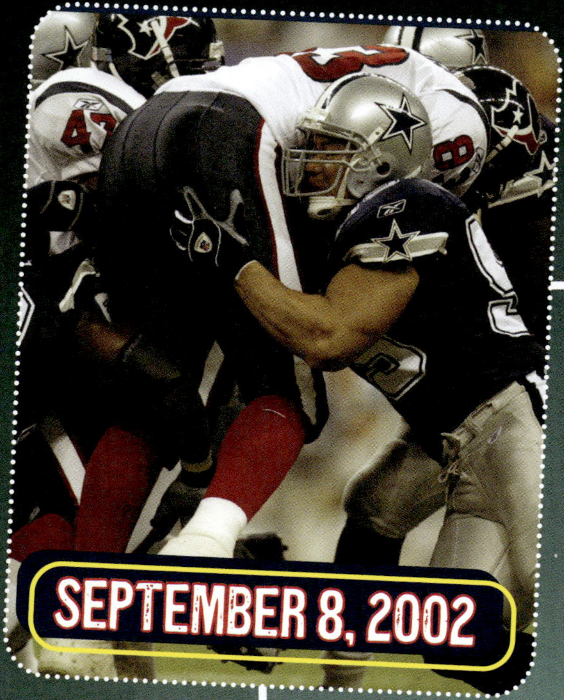

The Texans play their first game in franchise history and defeat the Dallas Cowboys 19–10.

The team earns its second playoff victory, a 19–13 win over the Cincinnati Bengals.

BIG DAYS

JANUARY 7, 2017

The Texans defeat the Oakland Raiders 27–14 in a wild card playoff game.

JANUARY 4, 2020

In a wild card playoff game, the Texans defeat the Bills 22–19.

MODERN-DAY MARVELS

Brandin Cooks

Wide Receiver | Debut: 2020

Cooks joined the Texans in 2020 after playing for the New Orleans Saints, New England Patriots, and Los Angeles Rams. In 2021, Cooks registered 1,037 receiving yards and caught six touchdown passes. It was the sixth season of his career with more than 1,000 yards.

Jonathan Greenard

Defensive End | Debut: 2020

Greenard played college football at Louisville University and the University of Florida. He was picked by the Texans in the third round of the 2020 NFL Draft. He totaled eight sacks and two forced fumbles during the 2021 season.

Davis Mills

Quarterback | Debut: 2021

The Texans selected Mills in the third round of the 2021 NFL Draft. As a rookie, he started 11 games for the team. He threw eight touchdown passes during the season's final four games. Mills finished with 2,664 yards passing and 16 touchdowns.

Laremy Tunsil

Offensive Tackle | Debut: 2019

Usually anchoring the left side of the offensive line, Tunsil has started every game he's played in his career. After three seasons with the Miami Dolphins, Tunsil joined the Texans for the 2019 season. His two Pro Bowl selections have come as a member of the Texans.

J. J. WATT WON THE NFL'S DEFENSIVE PLAYER OF THE YEAR AWARD THREE TIMES WHILE PLAYING FOR THE TEXANS.

THE GOAT

GREATEST OF ALL TIME

J. J. WATT

Watt created chaos on the line with his spectacular ability to rush the quarterback. Twice he led the league in sacks. His 20.5 sacks in 2012 and 2014 are tied for seventh-most in a single season since sacks became an official stat. He also led the league with seven forced fumbles in 2018. He led the league three times in tackles for a loss. Watt was selected for the Pro Bowl five times.

FAN FAVORITE

#1

Matt Schaub–Quarterback

2007–2013

As the team's starting quarterback, Schaub led the Texans to their first winning season ever in 2009. He also led the team to its first trip to the playoffs in 2011 and to its highest win total ever (12) in 2012. For these accomplishments, Schaub will forever have a place in the hearts of Houston fans.

THE BIG GAME

JANUARY 7, 2012

Coming into their wild card game against the Cincinnati Bengals, the Texans had never before competed in a playoff game. Midway through the second quarter, the Bengals led 10–7. But from there, the Texans scored the final 24 points of the game. Defensive end J. J. Watt returned an interception for a touchdown. Wide receiver Andre Johnson finished with 90 receiving yards and a touchdown. The star for the Texans, however, was running back Arian Foster. He rushed for 153 yards and two touchdowns. The Texans earned their first playoff victory, defeating the Bengals 31–10.

QUARTERBACK T. J. YATES LED THE TEXANS TO VICTORY IN THEIR FIRST-EVER PLAYOFF GAME.

BILL O'BRIEN LED THE TEXANS TO THE PLAYOFFS FOUR DIFFERENT TIMES.

AMAZING FEATS

396 Passes Completed

In 2009 by **QUARTERBACK** Matt Schaub

1,616 Rushing Yards

In 2010 by **RUNNING BACK** Arian Foster

1,598 Receiving Yards

In 2012 for **WIDE RECEIVER** Andre Johnson

13 Receiving Touchdowns

In 2017 for **WIDE RECEIVER** DeAndre Hopkins

ALL-TIME BEST

PASSING YARDS

Matt Schaub
23,221

Deshaun Watson
14,539

David Carr
13,391

RUSHING YARDS

Arian Foster
6,472

Domanick Williams
3,195

Lamar Miller
2,934

RECEIVING YARDS

Andre Johnson
13,597

DeAndre Hopkins
8,602

Owen Daniels
4,617

SACKS**

J. J. Watt
101

Whitney Mercilus
57

Mario Williams
53

SCORING

Kris Brown
767

Ka'imi Fairbairn
518*

Arian Foster
410

INTERCEPTIONS

Johnathan Joseph
17*

Kareem Jackson
16

Dunta Robinson
13

*as of 2021
**unofficial before 1982

TIGHT END OWEN DANIELS PLAYED EIGHT SEASONS FOR THE TEXANS FROM 2006 TO 2013.

GLOSSARY

division (dih-VIZSH-un): a group of teams within the NFL who play each other more frequently and compete for the best record

expansion team (ek-SPAN-shun TEEM): a new team added to the league

league (LEEG): an organization of sports teams that compete against each other

playoffs (PLAY-ahfs): a series of games after the regular season that decides which two teams play in the Super Bowl

Pro Bowl (PRO BOWL): the NFL's All-Star game where the best players in the league compete

sack (SAK): when a quarterback is tackled behind the line of scrimmage before he can throw the ball

stadium (STAY-dee-uhm): a building with a field and seats for fans where teams play

Super Bowl (SOO-puhr BOWL): the championship game of the NFL played between the winners of the AFC and the NFC

touchdown (TUTCH-down): a play in which the ball is brought into the other team's end zone, resulting in six points

FIND OUT MORE

IN THE LIBRARY

Bulgar, Beth and Mark Bechtel. *My First Book of Football.* New York, NY: Time Inc. Books, 2015.

Jacobs, Greg. *The Everything Kids' Football Book, 7th Edition*. Avon, MA: Adams Media, 2021.

Sports Illustrated Kids. *The Greatest Football Teams of All Time*. New York, NY: Time Inc. Books, 2018.

Wyner, Zach. *Houston Texans*. New York, NY: AV2 Books, 2020.

ON THE WEB

Visit our website for links about the Houston Texans:
childsworld.com/links

Note to parents, teachers, and librarians: We routinely verify our web links to make sure they are safe and active sites. Encourage your readers to check them out!

INDEX

ABOUT THE AUTHOR

Josh Anderson has published over 50 books for children and young adults. His two boys are the greatest joys in his life. Hobbies include coaching his sons in youth basketball, no-holds-barred games of Apples to Apples, and taking long family walks. His favorite NFL team is a secret he'll never share!